EDWARD L. ALBAN

THIS LIFE SO BRIEF BETWEEN ETERNITIES

POEMS

Copyright © 2023 by Edward L. Alban

All rights reserved. No part of this book may be reproduced in any manner whatsoever without written permission except in the case of brief quotations embodied in critical articles and reviews.

First Printing, 2023

THIS LIFE SO BRIEF BETWEEN ETERNITIES

~To JoAnn~

CONTENTS

Of Time and Words
1

New Year 2000
4

Autumn
7

The Aches of Time Within Our Psyche
8

Ageless Image
9

The Alarm Clock
10

Days
12

Intimations of Time
13

When News Arrives as History
19

Prairie Nocturne
20

CONTENTS

Sounds of Time
22

A Widower's Time Travel
23

Epiphanous Time
25

Time, the Matchmaker
26

Of Peace and Time
28

Robbing Oblivion
30

To a Poet of Renown
33

To Words, the Imps
35

One Golden Day
37

Between Eternities
39

The Eternity After Death
41

The Eternity Before Birth
46

Acknowledgements
53

CONTENTS

About The Author
54

OF TIME AND WORDS

The attic was a trove of family heirloom
Replete with books, contraptions and old toys.
More cemetery of things than storeroom,
It had grandfather's relics as a boy
Dilapidated artifacts and crafts
Exuding ages though the rafts.

I picked up oddities to inspect
Contraptions, relics from the past
And felt a condescending disrespect
For tools and toys that did not last
Junk jettisoned along the road of Time
Which was no longer worth a dime.

One item was a tapper for Morse Code
A gadget that back upon its day
Was swift communication á la mode
With fastest signals in relay.
How chic its operator must have been!
A well-paid techie of great esteem!

And yet, like many things around that room,
Their time of glory came and did not last.
The radio marked the tapper's doom
And turned him into an oddity of the past.
A Schumpeterian process was at play
Displacing old technologies away.

While looking through newspapers I found
A piece by Sidney Harris, a Chicago columnist
Who had collected jobs that were no longer 'round.

EDWARD L. ALBAN

He dared me pick an item from his list
And name the job it represented years ago.
I must confess that many I did not know.

Broderer, cogwainer, fletcher, girdler, horner, lorimer
Mercer, pavior, chandler, tyler, poulter, salter and skinner

It's odd how jobs and words share common fates.
They have their shining moment on the world stage
But then the scythe of time proceeds to obliterate
And heaps them with the rubble of an earlier age.
Job words come riding high on the new wave
Then crash upon oblivion's shores, impossible to save.

The Schumpeterian process builds and then destroys.
It brings new jobs but makes old ones effete.
As people train to adjust to new employs
Old ways succumb, becoming obsolete.
And words that rode the olden ways
Become discarded and perish in the fray.

The frumpy garb that served to adorn
The wild and heady days of years ago
Today elicits ridicule and scorn
Too prudish they, with hems too low.
And while apparel words may still endure
They're ghosts of something dead for sure.

The ruff, the corset, the bonnet
The stomacher, the farthingale
The tabards, bloomers and knickerbockers

It isn't only equipment and apparel that fade away
Ideologies and movements also come and go
And words that reigned with them in their day.
What happened to these systems of years ago:
feudalism, colonialism and utopianism?
Which is deader now: *communism or Nazism?*

The fate of words is tied to man's
And to the events that history betides.
Words follow man in caravans
Through the historic tides
Like stowaways on a ship
That perished on its final trip.

Not many things are here to stay.
Not even nations or the names they call themselves.
They change with the world's political fray
Like books relabeled and shifted on the shelves.
Where is the biblical kingdom of Philistia
And where, pray tell, is Elam or Cilicia?

Siam became Thailand, Bechuanaland became Botswana.
Rhodesia morphed onto Zimbabwe, Ceylon into Sri Lanka
And little Dutch Guinea renamed itself plain Suriname.

All this I understand, but what explains
The words that are not tied to things,
Such as the words on lips of swains
Upon the time of Tudor kings?
Words such as 'fie.'
Why did it have to die?

Why must quietus and contumely disappear?
This is a change I most deeply mislike.
If it was good enough for Shakespeare
Then what's there not to like?
These words are as elegant as the tabard
That once was worn by the old bard.

Methinks we should vouchsafe new life
To all those charming words of which
Elizabethan speech was rife.
We could still keep ours. No need to switch.
Pedantic though it may sound now
I wouldst use thee and thou enow!

NEW YEAR 2000

It was going on midnight and the room was full of celebrants,
Awaiting Old Man Time, champagne in hand
To catch him in the act of changing years.

To-night was very special as he would change
Not only years, but decades, centuries
And, zip-a-dee-doo-dah, even millennia!

Just think of all those nines in 1999 changing to zeros
And then that "1" which stood in first position for 1000 years
Would yield its place to a shiny "2," which would be in use
Till 2999, a date so deep in darkest future,
So deep that I can't even fathom.

But, ah, to be alive just then, with glass in hand
And toast the dawning at the cusp of history
And see the changing of the guard!

My mind was swirling with transcendental thoughts:
Mortality, infinity, humanity's existence.
Expecting that a moment of this magnitude
Was bound to make a splash for all to see
Perhaps with lights, perhaps with sounds
With breezy chills, or temblors from the ground.

And so, I searched the sky, looking for I didn't know what,
The final flicker of a dying star?
The nascent spark of a new one?
Or maybe even the specter of an hourglass up in the sky.

As midnight approached, excitement grew
Anticipation billowed to a tidal wave of expectation
And I could picture the final grains of sand scurrying down
The huge compartment of the hourglass
The very last of all those thousand years
Cascading down.

The crowds awaited like paparazzi stalking a celebrity,
Intent on capturing him on film.
The cameras were ready; camcorders were rolling.
The entire crowd in Times Square was gaping upwards,
Braving the cold night air, and waiting for time
To come riding the ball as it fell from 1999 to 2000.

It was then I thought I caught a glimpse
Of the sheen of the hourglass up in the sky
Its translucent, almost invisible surface
So fragile like the filament of a soap bubble
Iridescent only for a nanosecond.

Ah, to see the veil of Time among the stars
The membrane that envelops History
That holds the invisible sands of Time as they pass
From one compartment to another.
It would be flipping soon, to start spilling
Its cataracts of time into the 21st Century.

The count down at Times Square had already begun
I felt uplifted, levitated, floating upwards
Oh, that glorious soaring feeling!
Up, up and up I went ever rising,
Knowing that at midnight, Whoosh!
The hourglass would flip
And over the top we would all go!

And then it happened, but not as I expected.
There was no sudden drop
No roller coaster's plunging dive,
No bungee-jump precipitous freefall.
There wasn't any of that.

It was as smooth as a feather's gentle waft
That slid sideways on a ledge and comes to rest.

I felt nothing.
The whole thing was incommensurate with the hoopla
The revving up of madness and hyping expectations.
In fact, if I had been alone somewhere
I would have missed the whole thing.

But people were intent on making something out of it.
They jumped and screamed obstreperously
They blew their hoarse kazoos and tooting horns
And blew fireworks to add to the cacophony.

Like the intimation of a will-of-the-wisp
The hint of a vision that you more feel than see,
Time had disappeared like an invisible specter:
Seen by none but imagined by everyone!

We sat through the show of a great dodger,
We clenched our hands through the trumpet alarum,
We craned our necks during the drum roll,
But Time had conned us all.
He came and went as silent and invisible as ever.

My consolation was the memory
Of my imagined hourglass
Its diaphanous veil, glimmering so briefly
A diamond scintillating in the night
A pristine prism blushing under a shaft of light.

When the clamor abated, when the last refrain of Auld Lang Syne
Had faded into silence, there was a ratcheting sensation,
A feeling of having risen and come to rest without falling,
As if I'd just stepped off from a rising escalator onto
The floor at the bottom of a new millennium.

There, on the morning of January first,
I found myself, feeling sad, weary, (older!)
And sloshing on a puddle of time at
The bottom of a mostly empty hour-glass compartment.

AUTUMN

Arriving on a late September day
The autumn chill revved up my appetite,
Unleashing whims to dance, to romp and play
To run head-on against the wind's cold bite,
In search of love to end my days alone.
And then by one November night
The fall acquired a melancholy tone
And gripped my lonely heart so tight
I learned that autumn had another face:
No more the stunning leaves of red and gold
That promised love and set my heart ablaze
But russet withered leaves of wintry cold.
The golden glow of Fall just came to say:
"Hello, goodbye, I really cannot stay."

THE ACHES OF TIME WITHIN OUR PSYCHE

We are programmed
With letters, names and numbers
That shout the pain
Of hecatombs and injuries we lived.

The sound of 9-11 stirs a wound
Half cauterized by now.
And JFK and MLK make quiver
The placid membrane of our psyche
And Alamo and Pearl Harbor leave a
Distinctive taste of infamy.

But we, as individuals, also have
Insidious wounds from thefts and rapes
From jilts, rejections, and job firings.
These are without mnemonic letters
Without commemoration or parades.

Our own private misfortunes
Just rumble through our nerves
In seismic waves, that now and then
Erupt in fraught nightmares.
Yet happily, and differently enshrined,
We also have our precious times
When guardian angels intervened
And let us touch the sky
When luck smiled on us and poured bonanzas
When bolts of everlasting love struck us senseless
And victory elevated us to dizzying heights of glory.

AGELESS IMAGE

Our photo of thirty years ago
Made minor splashes at the time
Then was stuck away for years
And was forgotten.
Until we recently recovered it
And were surprised to see
The youthful image of the way we were
Our thin athletic bodies shining and glorious
Our rich bountiful hair, our skin magnolia-smooth
And all those attributes foregone
That mirrors now ungraciously belie.
Who says that mirrors can be trumped?
This photo is just the card for that.

THE ALARM CLOCK

He's electric these days
And works in silent ways.
His ticking has been muffled
To never again ruffle
His sleeper's calm.

Gone as well
Is his obnoxious bell
Which used to ring
As a mad bee sting
Upon your ears.

Now digits glow
In a continuous flow
Of phosphorescent lines
That morph in pantomimes
Upon a screen.

What's more you can sleep
Quite soundly and deep
Completely free to unwind
With peace of mind
Since he's in charge.

He has a battery pack
Around his back
In order to prevail
In case the power failed.
He thinks of everything.

Nor is there any harm
In sleeping past the alarm.
Just press a button on his head
And linger longer in your bed
He'll call you again.

Whatever you do, please
Don't overdo this.
Don't be a glutton
With the snooze button
Or you will press your luck.

He can take once, or twice
But three times is no dice.
He's an ogre by the third buzz
He'll raise an awful fuss
You'll definitely rue.

He'll shout beyond your ears
Till conscience herself hears
Unleashing a panic attack
That'll bolt you off the sack.
He'll sic guilt on you!

DAYS

Tomorrow stirs within the womb of time
Without arousing any excitement
As if the gift of life were déjà vu
As if a day were just another dividend
Of immortality that's now due.

Today is when the gift arrives.
It lasts twenty-four hours
And then it is forever gone.
And yet, I don't bestir myself to rise
And see the gift unwrapped at dawn.

The ship of time moves on, and *yesterday*
Retreats as flotsam in its wake
Inexorably drifting into history
Perhaps to reappear as one bright star
Within the firmament of memory.

Two days are marked upon our tombstone:
One heralds our tomorrows
Without a single yesterday
Another brims with yesterdays
And nary a one tomorrow.

INTIMATIONS OF TIME

I

So swift goes Time
I hardly notice it
Until it jolts me with a bill
For years consumed
I can't remember having lived
And I feel gypped.

Whole chapters of my life are blank
With days as if they never were
Accomplishments so few
They'd fill a thimble's worth.

But it's no use to question Time
He's always right.
My memory is at fault.

And so, I set to find
The scattered crumbs I left behind
To mark my trails.

Amid my trivia I find
Some photos, logs,
Scattered diaries and clippings
That serve as sparks
To light the catacombs
Of my forgotten years.

II

And, oh, what treasures I discover!
I am in Paradise regained
I'm young again.

I saunter in the splendor
Of golden summer days
Reviled by girls cavorting on the beach
Their bodies swaying with the waves.

In those invigorating raffish days
I flit from rose to rose
In search of promises of love.
And I was drunk with wanderlust
And famished for adventure
I would have roamed the corners of the earth.

 I dropped out of school to do my thing
To dabble in my dreams
A dilettante of this and that
With incompletes galore
I jingled immortality in my pockets
With millions of tomorrows.

III

And then I sensed
The stern reproof of Time.

"Keep on like this and you will have
But only a few Tomorrows
And they will be
Agonal and penurious.
Don't waste your youth, young man.
Make something of yourself."

His scorching words stung
But I just shrugged them off
And kept on having fun.

And Time saw fit to take a harsher tone.
"You still don't get it.
Just look at this."

He froze the world just like a video on pause
Where nothing moved, where birds stood
Suspended in mid flight
And people stood like statues

I saw my high school chums ahead
I could see John, an engineer
And there was Jim, a CPA
And Paul was out of medical school
My buddies all on track
To make their dreams come true
While I was lagging seven years behind
Adrift and lost.

I quickly quit my wasteful ways
And put more minutes in each hour than Time
Had ever known it had. I worked and worked
Until I reached my goal
And got my PhD.

IV

And now I'm sitting on a train
That has just left my eightieth birthday
And out the window I see
Our running shadow carpeting the ground
And deep within that moving blur
I sense the soul of Time

I dare to ask:
Should I be getting off before the next station?
"Not yet." I think He said.
(I hope I heard Him right).

Time's words are often unintelligible
At times he speaks in telepathic hints
Subliminally enlightening me
With magical epiphanies.

As in a day when visiting a cemetery
And seeing the names, the dates of births and deaths
A chilling thought conveyed these words:
In time, you too will be like them
Detritus by the path of Time.

Another time, while gazing at a starry sky
A vortex of ideas absorbed me to its depths
And ricocheting from conundrums to enigmas
I understood that Time confers the date
Of birth and death to everything under the sun
Except its own.
We do not know when Time began
Or if and when he'll end.

And once upon the gloaming of an evening
I caught the flash of His translucent skin
A membrane in space extending like
A shroud of history from eons ago
To infinity and beyond.

V

But most of all, I've sensed the aura of Time
In endings and beginnings
In births and deaths, in moments pregnant with
The joys and sorrows of life coming and going.

As when a new-born baby's cry
Evokes the passing of the gift of life
To younger generations
In a continuous marathon that's like
A virtual chain of human immortality.

And when I rise at dawn to greet another day
And hear the birds go all agog, exploding into song
They warble, trill and chirp and coo
As if they saw a baby of Time being born.

The glory of births is everywhere
I see it in a mighty river's birth upon a mountain top
Where crystal drops of dew confluence and collide
And slither all aglitter and bump and rush
Downhill to gather other drops, to turn to rivulets that ricochet
And splash and grow, becoming streams that roam the land
And soak it in a wet embrace.
I can just hear the piccolos and flutes
That mimic those scurrying drops
That Smetana so beautifully caught
In his *Moldau*.

VI

Alas, I also see the sadness in the end of things
Which always drag me to the depths of sorrow
I see the mighty river reach its end
Displaying dignity on seeing the delta ahead
It smells the brine and feels
Its fresh sweet water's end
And yet, it bravely meanders on
To meet the waiting gaping mouth
Of the colossal sea.

I'm also saddened by the visage of a cow
Being herded to the slaughterhouse
She marches innocent and meek
She looks at men, but no one says goodbye
I wish I had a clump of grass for her
But all that I can muster is a tear.

WHEN NEWS ARRIVES AS HISTORY

You came into my flickering life
And not a second late
Detained my fatal date.

You, the doctor on call;
and I, the afflicted child
with fever running wild.

While frantic relatives
could only cry and pray
you kept my death at bay.

But that was fifteen years ago.
Today I stand upon that same infirmary
Before a picture honoring your memory

Besieged with clashing feelings:
So glad to see you after all these years,
So sad for news that bring me tears.

I learned you died five years ago
And this vicissitude
Intrudes upon my gratitude.

I came to say hello
But death dropped by
And changed it to goodbye.

PRAIRIE NOCTURNE

The sky above a Kansas prairie
Upon a balmy summer night
Displays space so alive
Its cosmic plenitude stuns my senses.

Who would have thought the night
Could shame the day
By showing treasures that
The day, for all its light, kept hidden?

A myriad twinkling stars punctuate the dark
With peeping eyes that peek at me
From spangled constellations
While nebulae play hide-and-seek, and come and go
And fade from focus: foggy ghosts of the beyond.

Just then a breeze comes rushing through the hedges
With arms of veils that sway around me
And bring a redolence of fields and orchards
Of sweet and feminine scents I cannot place
Oh, what is it? Clover, lavender, or sage?

As I adjust to the night
The darkness pales, becoming friendlier,
I recognize more things for what they are
The wild cacophony is only crickets chirring
Or stuttering cicadas wildly in love
The eerie giant ogres of the dark are but
The staid silhouettes of stately cottonwoods.

The sky absorbs me in paradoxes
That take me a while to assimilate.
To think that some stars I saw
Could well be dead and gone by now.
So immense are distances
That even cruising at the speed of light,
Their living glow takes eons to get here.
It's hard to accept I'm looking at the past
I'm seeing the ghostly fire of one star
That died eons ago.

The sky absorbs my focus through
A tunnel that spirals to infinity
A sight so deep and dark it scares me
And humbles me to insignificance
I'm reeling in conundrums.

Thank Heaven for the stars
That taking pity on me
Intrude to rescue me from
Visions of the unfathomable
And shift my focus from the disorienting abyss.
I hear their calming voices in silent telepathic waves.

 "This is Andromeda speaking, can you see me?"
"And I am Cassiopeia, could you pronounce my name?"
"And we are the sirens of Orion, but now tell us
"Which is Rigel, which is Bellatrix, and which is Betelgeuse?"

The very sight of these stars is calming
They're ponderable, within a finite distance
Like islands in the night ahoy.
I linger in the night waiting for I-don't-know-what
Perhaps a muse galloping on a gust of wind
That comes to lead me to the depth of night
Where poems write themselves.
Who knows, perhaps tomorrow I'll find upon my desk
The rapturous stanzas of a nocturne scribbled inexplicably
By Bellatrix herself.

SOUNDS OF TIME

Invisible and often silent
Yet even so its presence
Is quite palpable.

Upon a storm I sense
The seconds splash,
Rambunctiously colliding in the spray.

And then in cemeteries
Its solemn steps vanish discreetly
As tears slithering on tiptoes.

Before the pyramids or Roman aqueducts
I hear its praises whistling in the wind:
Imagine this standing for millennia!

Before the Tetons or Grand Canyon
It hear it in my sighs that gasp in awe
For mother nature's Art.

A WIDOWER'S TIME TRAVEL

He awakened from a nap and relished
The sweet, beguiling remnants of
A dream that now enlivened his dull
Lethargic afternoon with memories of days
When lust for life ran torrents through his veins.

Ebullience such as this came only in dreams.
Awake, the old man's memories evoked
At best jejune recalls devoid of punch.

To vivify his memories, he gathered
Albums, pictures, clippings from old days
And came upon a photograph of his
Late wife when she was thirty-something.

A flame out of its frame
She brought the fire he sought
Absorbing him, transporting him
To worlds he loved where he
Could feel her breath
And hear the murmur of her sighs
And smell the lavender she loved.

He studied every feature
Her golden hair that framed her face
Her lips, slightly stretched, hinting a smile
Her eyes, bewitching stars, besotting him with love.

Fate had dropped her on his arms
And given him the happiest years of his life.
But then, inscrutably, it'd repossessed her
By taking her too suddenly, too soon
Out of this world.

This picture was the sparkling glass slipper
His lovely Cinderella left behind
It was alive with vivid reminiscences.

He looked at it for hours
But by the second day
The magic dissipated.
It had a Midas curse.
It raised insatiable longings
That left him thirsting, wanting more.

He grasped at love he could not have
He flayed his arms in vain
His fingers clawed thin air
He reached to touch a ghost
Who could not love him back.

In time, the picture hurt
It brought despair and tears
And he resolved to rid himself of it
If only temporarily.

He stuck it in a box
Not bothering to mark it
Like burying a treasure
Without a map.

Oh, yes, he'd look for it again
That was the ritual.
The day would come
When just the search alone
Would be an adventure.
A quest for thrills
For youth, for love!

EPIPHANOUS TIME

When all directions of escape are closed
And all the three dimensions lead nowhere
When you feel lost or trapped, remember:
There is a fourth dimension yet
Intangible, invisible, and silent.
It is the last recourse to your despair.

It's an epiphany of hope and promise
A vivid rainbow ablaze on your horizons
That brings salvation soon
If not this hour, the next
If not today, tomorrow.

Just sit and think.
Inspect and analyze! Scheme and plot!
And look for fissures in the walls
For weak points in your prison
For ways to call for help
For ways to keep alive.

If nothing else, take comfort in the fact
That time is on your side.
And Time may set you free
As many men have been
Who were condemned to die
And then exonerated at the eleventh hour.

TIME, THE MATCHMAKER

A quiet urban idyll in one big city park
Contains a bench surrounded by rose bushes
Umbrellaed by a sycamore tree.

As people come and go at different hours
The lifeless scene becomes a stage for worlds
As far apart as distant universes
With no wormholes connecting them.

At 9 am a widow walks her dog
And takes her daily rest
Upon the solitary bench.

At 1 pm a secretary sits for lunch
Enjoying peace and solitude
While dreaming of Prince Charming.

At 4 pm a hobo arrives and claims it as
His living-room, inviting birds and squirrels
For afternoon tea.

At 6 pm a banker passes by
And misses the secretary
Whom he'd have met if he had come at 1.

At 9 pm drug dealers with their bodyguards
Transact their business and exchange
Their bads for money.

The habitués don't know the different worlds
Their private nook becomes in their absence.
Steve and Mary come and go, but never meet
Remaining unaware of
The other's existence.

But they are bound to meet.
The Gods of love are working on it.
They've brought them to this park already
But have not managed the right time.
They're making progress.

And then, success at last!
Mary, the secretary, and Steve the banker meet.
It was not where you might think.
It was abroad while on vacation
Ten thousand miles from home.

They couldn't believe they came
So far away to meet.
They missed each other for so long
While being so close
And now so far from home
In serendipitous togetherness.

They met in *El Retiro* Park, Madrid!
For this occasion, Time himself played usher
And led Steven through the park directly to
The bench where Mary sat.

If love's to be, it'll happen anywhere
In distant continents of Earth
But Time has got to be on board.

Madrid did get it all together
With such a splash that Steve and Mary
Fell madly in love and wed forever after.

OF PEACE AND TIME

The epic Pyrrhic battles, the atrocious inhumanities of WWII
Are now forgotten and relegated to film archives and movies.
Who could believe that those atrocious and abominable foes
Japan and Nazi Germany, would be our staunch allies today,
Our friends and trading partners?

There's an important lesson here. Enduring peace is not
A mere cessation of hostilities, extended armistice
Or fighting that has stopped.
Peace comes from arduous work
It needs to be created, crafted, molded
Strengthened, nurtured until Time
Confirms that it is true and real.

When winners of a war are despotic, vengeful autocrats
We get no peace. We get an epoch of Cold War
A period of simmering discontent, of latent distrust
With vibes and fumes that brew a future war.

But when the winners are compassionate, humane
And wisely help rebuild their enemies,
Old animosities succumb to camaraderie
And peace takes root and grows.

The allies who won the war instilled respect
For human rights and freedom
For rule of law and democratic institutions.
The fruits of peace came flourishing in arts
In education, industry, in science and sports.
They fostered peace.
We are the living proof of what good victors can achieve.
I praise wholeheartedly the men who fought and won the war
And, those who ensured the peace.

ROBBING OBLIVION

A photo from late 1800s shows an old
And moldy building bulldozed ages ago.
A group is posing on its front steps
In frumpy garb, and odd hairstyles
Like aliens from another age.

I enter their world
And come alive in their time
Intruding like a specter from the future
Invisible to them, slithering among them
And breathing the sunny morning air
Of one bright day in early Spring
Before I ever was.

As I study them, they become
More human, more familiar
I hear their snickers and their mumbles
Their whispers, their laughter and their grumbles.
They are no longer freaks
Nor aliens but Americans
They're ordinary people, bosses
Coworkers, parents, friends and secretaries
And I suspect, that two are lovers, too.
I catch the vibes between them
Their coy and youngish smiles.

Then suddenly I hear a photographer
Intoning his instructions: Say cheese, at one...at two...
And then a bulb goes pop with bursting incandescence
That's swallowed by the camera in the wink of a shutter.

THIS LIFE SO BRIEF BETWEEN ETERNITIES

This shouldn't startle me anymore.
And yet, it sends me in transcendental wanderings
Transporting me to a world before my birth
Before the time photography existed
When Old Man Time
Unceremoniously threw away
The precious moments of the hour.
No matter how important
Or how historically significant
The moments were, they went to waste
Because there was no means to save them.
They simply were routinely handed to oblivion.

The advent of the camera changed that.
It turned a moment into a living thing
A slice of life which could be saved
By simply capturing
The membrane of a second
Entrapping it in film
With all the people and their clothes
Their hairstyles,
Their frowns and their smiles.

I saw how all this happened
I could see Old Man Time scooping up
The moment of the hour and then
Delivering it to the Goddess of Oblivion
Who'd dump it in her waste bin.

Just then the Promethean Louis Daguerre
Shows up out of nowhere.
He is chasing Old Man Time shouting:
"No! No! Please don't waste it. Give it here."

The Goddess of Oblivion is alarmed
And urges Time to ignore Daguerre.
She is flaying her arms, pleading, shouting:
"Hurry, hurry Time! Give it to me.
I'll hold it and I'll never share it.
I will dispose of it. Give it to me!"

And just as Old Man Time is reaching for Oblivion's hands
Daguerre, snatches it from him and passes it to
Another Goddess who has just come into the scene,
The Goddess of Posterity.

Posterity now holds the treasure proudly
And raises it high above her head for all to see.
She struts a little victory walk and says:
"I have the treasure now. It's safe with me.
I will keep it forever and share it with the world!"

Then, suddenly, Posterity hands it to me and disappears.
I find myself back in my own time stunned
And holding the sepiated picture in my hand
A window to a world that came alive for me
And took me back in time to see
The constancy of humanity.

Forget the superficial nuances of dress
Of hair style and fashions.
They come and go.
But fundamental facts endure.
A smile and love, as I just learned,
Will always have that feel
Of one warm ray of sunshine.

TO A POET OF RENOWN

Your poetry is a labyrinth
Of convoluted verses and stanzas
Where adjectives hang jerry-rigged
On wobbly structures and crooked facades.

It's a strange village of words
Where I meander disoriented
Along streets and alleyways
That lead me to dead ends.

Suddenly, you appear
Sauntering in parade
Like a proud emperor on a victory walk,
Strutting through the streets, bowing, waving,
Thanking your subjects, your admirers, your readers
While I stand back dumbfounded, asking myself:
Is it only me? Am I the only one who sees the
Poet emperor completely naked?

I'm told you are really dressed in the finest haberdashery
Of metaphors and similes;
Your garments are veils of gilded gossamer,
But all I see is tropes of extravagantly contorted meaning,
Jabberwocky of mysterious connotations with triple entendre
That you claim, as a poet, you have a license to use.

Some of these lines have a nice ring to them,
As in: knives of fire that cut water,
Stony cat whiskers that make flinty mustaches
Naked moons; dead birds in tree branches.

I'm lost. What world do you live in?
I've never seen such things!

TO WORDS, THE IMPS

I was trying to honor words with an ode and begged for help with rhyme. They refused. I took revenge on them and wrote:

> In dictionaries they appear from A to Z
> All in formation, eager aides to be
> Giving the impression they are dutiful slaves,
> But they are really arrant knaves
> Most often not subservient
> Extremely disobedient.
> They fail to come when they are called.
> They dally, they hide and stall,
> Like ornery little whelps
> Who just refuse to help.
> At other times the opposite is true.
> They flirt with writers, and they coo
> They volunteer for duty at no pay
> They clamor for a role to play
> They'll be in your show at all costs
> As stars or even host!

Not counting on help from the impish words, I had to write my ode to them entirely without rhyme:

> Words...scribbles lining paragraphs
> Like seedlings in the furrows of a field
> And blooming into gardens
> In the expanses of the soul.
>
> Words... phonemes and morphemes
> That flow in cadences and rhymes
> To resonate within the heart

And titillate the intellect.

Words... inchoate tiles in a linguistic mosaic
Holding their own upon a page
And waiting for the reader's mind
To unfold the mural's scape.

Words... filigrees of language
Golden gems adorning
Silver pendants holding
The garments of a thought.

Words...doves in flight
Aflutter in verses
Carrying utterances of the heart
On their wings.

How I begged for rhyme in the stanzas above! But words are so capricious at times. They just refused me and said: not now, my Love. And so, I left my verses without rhymes.

ONE GOLDEN DAY

All I can do is see that day for what it was,
No more no less,
Just a perfect moment in time
A mother strolling with her handsome sons.
　　　　　—"A Moment Caught in Time," Joanne Jagoda

I

I intrude into the impossible
And bask upon the sunshine of a day
Before I ever was
A day some years before
The cataclysmic World War II
A day of calmness
A day of child-like innocence
Without a care or fear
Still suffused with peace and joy
All I can do is see that day for what it was.

II

Don't ask if it was May or August
Or Monday or Friday
Because it was a day so ordinary
Nobody bothered to record the facts
But for this photograph
That stole one golden moment
And managed to preserve it

through war and all
and all the decades since
no more no less.

III

This day was made in Heaven
But it was lived right here on Earth
In Hamburg, Germany 'round 1932
When Nazi devils were already afoot
Just standing by, dissembling,
Preparing, gaining power in sheep's clothing
While lambs frolicked in leas among the daffodils
And didn't suspect a thing
It was a golden day, ah just
A perfect moment in time.

IV

It was a time when Jews could stroll
Through downtown Hamburg
With pride in their smiles
Without the opprobrium of
The Star of David branded on their faces
And sewn to their clothing
So, here's my dad-to-be strolling
 With his twin and in between
None other but my grandma killed at Auschwitz
A mother strolling with her handsome sons.

BETWEEN ETERNITIES

Before birth: the darkness of the womb.
Beyond death: the darkness of the tomb.
From dark to dark we go
Life shining for a second and then lo
Just blinking. A spark
Between eternities of dark.

For millions of years before birth
And millions after death
Existence is forlorn:
We're dead, or yet unborn.
And yet, a life so brief
Consumes me in neither ire nor grief.

That Providence could only spare
A measly breath of air
A mere second of life
Where eons and eons were rife
Should bring me much resentment
And yet, I only feel contentment.

I don't feel cheated
Or defeated.
I will not mount a strife
Against short-shifted life.
I just accept what cannot be
And that's enough for me.

I do not live as if in wait
To be reborn at heaven's gate.
This life, not far indefinite tomorrows
Holds all my joys and sorrows.
I've come to terms with my mortality,
And its implacable finality.

This brief and inexplicable interlude
That brashly dares to intrude
Upon eternities of lifelessness
So fills my life with happiness
That I rejoice each day
I live day after day.

THE ETERNITY AFTER DEATH

I

That end of ends that death portends
That final cataclysm 'round the bend
Truncating our lifespan
Has always bothered man
For being a curse
Without recourse.

It is an awful deal
That man cannot appeal.
No king with all his horses
Has ever beat fate's forces.
Man's consolation prize
Was only a compromise.

In lieu of nothing after death
Man took the promise of rebirth
Accepting transmigration
Metempsychosis, reincarnation
A land of honey and manna.
A Heaven, a Nirvana.

Because nobody could return from death to expose
That Heaven didn't exist or smell of rose
There was no way
That anybody could gainsay
The claims for paradise
And prove them otherwise.

II

It came to pass that faith
Became man's shibboleth
Eternal life was his to live
But only if he believed
But if he abjured,
It was eternal death for sure.

Like rainbow's end with pots of gold
The promised afterlife took hold
Incentivizing man with hope
And helping him to cope
With all the world's ordeals
With ills that would not heal.

At first, the concept lacked the specs
The costs, the frills, and perks.
How much was man entitled to?
What would he need to do?
Would everybody qualify?
Much had to be specified.

The Church, an institution of rising eminence,
Emerged to speak for Providence
And it proclaimed in one decree
That Heaven wouldn't be free!
The price for Heaven after death
Was good behavior on this Earth.

III

And good behavior meant
A tithe, in worldly cents,
Church loyalty
And fealty.
Rewards galore would come
In your celestial home.

For sacrifices such as martyrdom
Rewards could be obscenely handsome:
A harem with virgins all afire
To sate the martyr's lewd desires
With girls doting on him
To grant him every whim.

A pauper could be king
A ruler of everything.
Whatever he wished was his
Since Heaven aimed to please.
His funds could cover any check
His cards were from a magic deck.

He could become a living thing
A flower, tree, or spring.
Reincarnating into a creature
Of very different features
Or he could turn to a spectral being,
A shadow of himself with wings.

IV

For me, reincarnation is a poor prize.
It gives you life, but none you'd recognize.
Would you come back as a disgusting rat?
Is life so dear you would stoop to that?
I wouldn't come back as anything but me
And I would chuck it all if that couldn't be.

Man is the only living creature
With this especial feature:
His body alone is mortal
His soul is blessedly immortal.
His body and soul will separate
Upon arrival at the pearly gate.

And so, if you believed
You'll die, but still, you'll live.
Good souls will dwell
In Heaven. Bad souls in hell.
But much of this I just can't buy
It's too contrived to live by.

I don't believe that we can cleave apart
A man to mortal and immortal parts
Any more than we can separate *Me* from *I*
Allowing one to live, the other die.
For me, the whole of man will rot
And turn to naught.

V

There is no life beyond this earth
No hell, no heaven, no rebirth.
There's only nothingness
An empty darkness
Exactly what we had before being born
When Death was simply being unborn.

Can immortality be gained through fame?
Some claim they are the same
And they insist:
If you're remembered, you'll exist,
Ignoring that the world may toast to you and sing
But if you're dead, you will not hear a thing.

Eternity is too long
To not pall on.
I can't imagine being enthralled
That long at all.
Why bother looking ahead
Beyond the time I'm dead?

Poor thing, I hear some people say
With great dismay.
"How can he accept the thought
That all will come to naught?
How can he countenance
Eternal death with nonchalance?"

THE ETERNITY BEFORE BIRTH

I

Ah, pity me not. I am at peace.
I face eternal nothingness with ease
Because this life, short as it is,
Has given me immeasurable bliss.
And while the time I have to live
Is fixed and has no give

It's also true that I can change its depth
That I can change its breadth
And can vicariously tack on
The life of others to my own
Absorbing written history
Reliving others' memory.

Why fault the shortness of it all
When life at hand is such a ball?
Why not enjoy the here and now that's real
Instead of Heaven's iffy ideal?
Why drive yourself deranged
With things you cannot change?

For me, existence past the day we die
Is nothing but a big white lie.
But others embrace the lie without fail
Because without it, they simply couldn't prevail.
But I accept that once you're gone
You're forever done.

II

Forget what you might be after you're dead
That is so unimportant! But think instead
About those yet to come. The future is theirs.
It's they who should be in your prayers.
So, change your point of view.
The distant future isn't really about you.

I focus on the here and now
And on the riches that the past endows.
There is so much to explore
So much that came before:
The rise and fall of nations
Of cultures and civilizations.

Like an attic where we store
Our heritage, our roots, our lore
World history is a theater of the past
That features our ancestors in its cast
And offers worlds to be regained
To resurrect and live again.

III

We read of people whom we homage
We live their years, but never age.
We broaden our longevity by piling on
The experiences of others to our own
And thus, I feel as if I've grown tenfold.
I am a young eight-hundred-year-old!

Through books and films, I can compile a show
Of life before my birth and come to know
The world I missed. This doesn't lengthen my lifespan
But does extend its breadth and depth, and does expand

The quality of my life; I don't get older, only wiser.
That's how I cheat longevity, the miser.

It is the past's munificence
That compensates my brief existence
That loosens up the grip of my fatality
And lets me taste a sort of immortality
By taking me to worlds that I hold dear
Where I hobnob with Shakespeare.

For me, a grievous crime
Is waste of time.
It is my dedicated strife
To shun it from my life.
Some days I fail, and when I do
That is the hell I rue.

IV

To see the future, I look behind
Not with my eyes, but with my mind.
I look at Tuesday out of Wednesday's window,
And hardly ever out of Monday's window.
By Wednesday, Tuesday will be yesterday.
It costs a day, but hindsight saves the day.

This gets a little trickier for longer times ago.
Go back 100 years. Stop. Look home again and lo!
From that perspective, our present time
Is like a future dream sublime
It lets me see 2017 with 1917 eyes
And leaves me wildly mesmerized.

Absorb yourself in 1917
Then come to 2017 through all the years between
Imagine what people from 100 years ago
Would give to know what we now know.
So many events to be discerned
So much to live and learn.

By looking through 1917 eyes
Today is unbelievable. I am a-gush with sighs!
As Earth plods on in orbit and revolves
The sweep of history unfolds. The world evolves!
This God-like power makes me feel
Omniscient as I move through time at will.

V

This magic power is not unique to our generation
Ancestors also enjoyed a similar situation.
They too could see the cards their predecessors had
And knew when they were good or bad.
Like us, they looked below from their mountain top
At earlier generations attempting to look up.

Can't see one hour beyond your death?
Then have ten centuries before your birth!
The greatest recompense
For blindness of times hence
Is going back in time to see today
Become a glorious future day!

This feature of the Past, this God-like vantage point
Is mostly gratifying, but it can also disappoint
As when the bigger picture allows us to perceive
The injustices of fate that hapless men received.
They lived in penury, in misery, through hell!
And riches after death can't make that well.

The men, usually artists, lived in misery
Misfits that struggled to survive in penury.
Working for nothing but the love of art
Talented paupers with a golden heart
Who abnegated the materialistic life
To martyr in a noble strife.

VI

Here is the irony that their situations raise.
Once dead, the world saw fit to lavish praise,
To pour great wealth, honor, and fame
Upon their work and name.
Their paintings and sculptures rose in price
Some winning posthumously a prize.

Why hold the praise and fortune
To times so inopportune?
I cringe every time I hear the sum one pays
For a Van Gogh these days.
They go for millions, extravagant amounts
That poor Van Gogh couldn't even start to count.

It's easy to blame the fates for this,
By all appearances they were remiss.
Poor Vincent, in life he never got his due
And then in death, he got belated overdo.
His work ignored, dealers diddled and stood by
As if waiting for his death before rushing to buy.

A pauper in life, in death a multi-millionaire
A posthumous artist extraordinaire
Van Gogh was spared having to wonder
If it was all an accident or providential blunder.
But we, with our God-like view of the long run
Can see the tardy ways of fate and are stunned.

VII

Fate's ways are inscrutable,
Unjust, intractable
With much out of purview
And little we can do!
The past we cannot change.
The future's out of range.

We plant a seed, but will not see
The acorn as a tree.
And yet, we're part of what we will not see
We touch a world in which we will not be.
This Earth remains the common stage
That hosts our lives age after age.

We come and go but what we do endures
The good, the bad; the clean the impure.
As stewards of this endangered planet
We should do something now. At least just plan it!
We're tenants of this Earth and only borrow
What's destined for tomorrow.

We must desist in all the depredations
And make it better for future generations.
Calamity and catastrophe draw near
The day of reckoning is practically here.
So let the future say of us: our deeds were the best present
We could have ever sent.

ACKNOWLEDGEMENTS

Edward L. Alban writes: *I have attended many writing conferences. I have memories of good times and people. But I can only think of those at The Writer's Hotel as endeavors that were fruitful and productive in the sense that they led me to improve my work, or to even create poems that I gleaned from having attended the workshop.*

Edward L. Alban (Eddie to friends and colleagues) was born in Ecuador in 1938. He settled in Savannah, Georgia in 1952, and married his wife JoAnn in 1965. They raised two children together. A professor of Economics, he has taught at Auburn University, SUNY Potsdam, Armstrong State University and Savannah State University. He retired in 2000 and has been writing poetry and fiction ever since.

In his retirement, he and JoAnn have traveled throughout Europe and South America, pursuing his new avocation for languages and literature and publishing poetry, fiction and nonfiction.

Other published works by Edward L. Alban:
"Word Memoirs" (Independently published, 2022)
"Our Gun Idolatry" (Independently published, 2018)
"Stealing Forbidden Dreams" (Alban Books, 2023)

For more information about Edward Alban, please visit his website at www.luiseduardoalban.com

www.ingramcontent.com/pod-product-compliance
Lightning Source LLC
Chambersburg PA
CBHW050728010526
44107CB00009B/777